Growing Readers

New Hanover County Public Library

Purchased with
New Hanover County Partnership for Children
and Smart Start Funds

Who Grows Up in the Snow?

**A Book About
Polar Animals
and Their Offspring**

**Written by Theresa Longenecker
Illustrated by Melissa Carpenter**

Content Advisor: Julie Dunlap, Ph.D.
Reading Advisor: Lauren A. Liang, M.A.
Literacy Education, University of Minnesota
Minneapolis, Minnesota

Editor: Peggy Henrikson
Designer: Melissa Voda
Page production: The Design Lab
The illustrations in this book were prepared digitally.

Picture Window Books
5115 Excelsior Boulevard
Suite 232
Minneapolis, MN 55416
1-877-845-8392
www.picturewindowbooks.com

Printed in the United States of America.
1 2 3 4 5 6 08 07 06 05 04 03

Library of Congress Cataloging-in-Publication Data
Longenecker, Theresa, 1955–
  Who grows up in the snow? : a book about polar animals and their offspring / written by Theresa
Longenecker ; illustrated by Melissa Carpenter.
    p. cm.
  Summary: Names and describes the offspring of a polar bear, seal, emperor penguin, arctic fox, walrus,
caribou, arctic tern, and arctic hare.
  ISBN 1-4048-0028-X (lib. bdg. : alk. paper)
  1. Zoology—Polar regions—Juvenile literature. [1. Zoology—Polar regions.] I. Carpenter, Melissa, ill.
II. Title.
  QL104 .L66 2003
  599.139—dc21
                                                                                        2002006279

In some places in the world, the ground is covered with snow and ice most, or even all, of the year. Many baby animals grow up in the snow. Some survive by staying with their parents. Others grow up quickly and take care of themselves.

Let's read about some baby animals that grow up in the snow.

Pup

A baby harp seal is called a pup.

This seal pup was born on a floating ice pack. The seal pup was yellow at first, but in two days it turned snowy white. The pup will stay close to its mother for a few weeks more. It will drink her milk and grow stronger.

Did you know?
Pups start to swim when they are only three weeks old.

Chick

A baby emperor penguin is called a chick.

Emperor penguin chicks are born one at a time. As soon as the mother lays the egg, the father penguin rolls it onto his feet. His belly and feathers warm the egg. After hatching, the chick has a cozy spot to stand.

Did you know?
The chick often gets its first food from its father.

Calf

A baby walrus is called a calf.

When a walrus calf is two days old, it goes with its mother to join other mothers and calves on the shore. These groups are called nursery herds. Within a month, all the calves learn how to swim.

Did you know?
In the water, the calf often rides between its mother's front flippers. The calf also rides on its mother's back.

Cub

A baby polar bear is called a cub.

These twin polar bear cubs were born in a snow cave. They drink their mother's milk and will depend on her until they are almost two years old. They learn how to catch fish and hunt so they can live on their own.

Pup

A baby arctic fox is called a pup.

Arctic fox pups are born in a den underground. These pups snuggle into their mother's bushy tail to stay warm. Their father brings food to their mother. She can't leave the den while the pups are nursing.

Did you know?
In the spring when the pups are born, the mother arctic fox is light brown. The newborn pups are darker brown. In the winter, all arctic foxes turn white to blend with the snow.

14

Calf

A baby caribou is called a calf.

An hour after birth, a caribou calf can stand on its own and follow its mother. Like its mother, the calf has large hooves. The hooves spread out and keep the calf from sinking into the snow or soft ground.

Chick

A baby arctic tern is called a chick.

As soon as these arctic tern chicks hatch, they leave the nest. They hide nearby among the rocks and shore plants. Their parents bring them fish to eat. After a few weeks, the chicks are able to fly.

18

Leveret

A baby arctic hare is called a leveret.

Leverets are born covered with warm fur. They are ready to move about right away. The nest for these babies is just a dip in the ground. The mother lines the nest with grass and her own soft fur.

Did you know?
A mother arctic hare stays with her babies for the first two to three days. Then she visits once a day to nurse them for only a few minutes at a time.

Fast Facts

Harp Seal: Seal pups drink lots of milk and gain weight quickly. They grow a layer of blubber, or fat, that protects them from the cold. At three weeks, they start to swim and feed themselves. Pups are born with all of their teeth. When they have finished nursing, they use their sharp teeth to tear food apart. Harp seals have a coat of waterproof fur that keeps them warm. They get their name from the dark harp shape on their backs.

Emperor Penguin: After laying her egg, the mother penguin goes swimming and looking for fish. The father takes care of the egg for about eight weeks. He doesn't eat anything all that time. After the chick is born, the father makes a milk-like liquid in his throat and spits it up into the chick's mouth. When the mother returns, the father goes off to hunt. On land, a penguin waddles, hops, and toboggans on its tummy. In the water, it can swim fast and dive very deep.

Walrus: Female walruses give birth to a single calf. The newborn weighs as much as a grown person. A mother walrus takes care of her calf for two years. After that, the calf can find food on its own. It has stiff whiskers that help it feel for food on the dark ocean floor. A walrus loves clams and also eats crabs, shrimp, snails, and fish. A calf's tusks appear during its first summer or fall. A walrus can use its tusks like ice picks to cut a hole in the ice or to pull its heavy body up out of the water.

Polar Bear: Newborn polar bear cubs are tiny compared to their parents. A cub weighs only one pound (one-half kilogram) when it is born and is little more than one foot (30 centimeters) long. Males are full-grown at four years old, while females reach their full size between the ages of three and seven. An adult female polar bear can weigh 500 pounds (227 kilograms), and a male can weigh well over 1,000 pounds (454 kilograms).

Arctic Fox: There are usually 6 to 10 arctic fox pups in a litter. The family stays together over the summer. The pups go their own way in the fall. During summer, the foxes store up food for the cold winter. They eat small animals, birds, berries, fish, and seal meat left by bears. Arctic foxes use their long, bushy tails like scarves to keep their noses warm when they lie down.

Caribou: Each spring, female caribou leave the herd and go to the same place to have their calves. Each mother has only one calf. At birth, a calf weighs about 13 pounds (6 kilograms). It doubles its weight in 10 to 15 days. Soon, the mothers and calves join the herd again. Caribou herds can walk miles each day looking for food. Caribou eat grasses, mushrooms, moss, and lichen growing on rocks and trees.

Arctic Tern: Arctic terns nest in colonies of up to 50 birds. A mother tern lays one to three eggs at a time. The nest might be on grass, sand, or bare rocks. Both parents take care of the eggs and feed the chicks. When a chick is three months old, it can migrate, or fly south for the winter. Arctic terns migrate halfway around the world—the farthest of any bird. They have webbed feet like ducks, but they don't swim well. They spend most of their time in the air. Besides fish, arctic terns eat insects, shrimp, and tiny, shrimp-like krill.

Arctic Hare: Arctic hares have between one and eight leverets at a time. The mother hare's milk is very rich in fat, so the babies don't need to nurse often. Arctic hares often gather in groups to keep warm, feed, or protect themselves from enemies. In the far north, these groups can be as big as 200 to 300 hares. Arctic hares feed on twigs, roots, berries, mosses, and grasses. These hares can run very swiftly and can hop on their hind legs like kangaroos.

Polar Babies at a Glance

Word for Baby	Animal	Born How	First Food	Word for Female	Word for Male	Word for Group
Pup	Harp seal	Live	Mother's milk	Female	Male	Herd
Chick	Emperor penguin	Egg	Milk-like fluid the father coughs up	Female	Male	Rookery
Calf	Walrus	Live	Mother's milk	Cow	Bull	Herd, pod
Cub	Polar bear	Live	Mother's milk	Female	Male	——
Pup	Arctic fox	Live	Mother's milk	Vixen	Reynard	Leash, skulk
Calf	Caribou	Live	Mother's milk	Cow	Bull	Herd
Chick	Arctic tern	Egg	Small fish, krill	Female	Male	Colony
Leveret	Arctic hare	Live	Mother's milk	Doe	Buck	——

Where Do They Live?

Harp seal—along the coasts of the North Atlantic and Arctic Oceans

Emperor penguin—Antarctica and the cold southern oceans

Walrus—northern Pacific and Atlantic oceans

Polar bear—in and around the Arctic Ocean

Arctic fox—arctic areas around the North Pole

Caribou—far northern forests and plains of North America, Europe, and Asia

Arctic tern—breeds in the Arctic (around the North Pole) but flies all the way to the Antarctic (around the South Pole) every year

Arctic hare—northern Canada, the Arctic islands, and Greenland

Fun with Fat!

Fat, or blubber, keeps many snow animals warm. Let's see if it does the same for you.

What You Need

Medium-size bowl

5 ice cubes

Cold water

A plastic sandwich bag

Shortening

A thin rubber glove

What to Do

1. Put the ice cubes into the bowl, then fill it half full of cold water.
2. Fill the plastic bag about half full of shortening.
3. Put on the rubber glove.
4. Put your gloved hand into the bag of shortening until your fingers are covered.
5. Place your hand with the bag on it into the ice water until the water covers your fingers. (Don't let water get into the bag.) How does that feel?
6. Now take your hand out of the glove and put your bare fingers into the bowl of ice cubes and cold water. Does the cold water feel different this time? How?

Words to Know

blubber—a thick layer of fat just under the skin of many snow animals. Blubber keeps them warm.

colony—a group of the same animals living together. Arctic terns live in colonies when they nest.

harp—a musical instrument that has a curved top. The harp seal got its name because of the harp shape on its back.

krill—sea creatures that look like tiny shrimp

lichen—tiny plants that grow on trees and rocks

migrate—to travel from one area to another. Some animals migrate to a particular place every year to mate, feed, or have babies.

nurse—to drink mother's milk

tusk—a very long, pointed tooth that sticks out when the mouth is closed. A walrus's tusks can be used for fighting, cutting through ice, or pulling itself up out of the water.

To Learn More

At the Library

Baker, Alan. *The Arctic.* Chicago: Peter Bedrick Books, 1999.

Butterfield, Moira. *Animals in Cold Places.* Austin, Tex.: Raintree Steck-Vaughn, 2000.

Holmes, Kevin, J. *Penguins.* Mankato, Minn.: Bridgestone Books, 1998.

On the Web

Want to learn more about polar baby animals? Visit FACT HOUND at *http://www.facthound.com.*

Index